Coscom
Entertainment

CAUGHT IN BLACK HEADLIGHTS

A.P. Fuchs

COSCOM ENTERTAINMENT
WINNIPEG

The poems in this book are just that: poems. Names, characters, places and events either are products of the author's imagination or are used fictitiously. Any resemblance to actual events or persons living or dead or who died for poetic justice is purely coincidental.

ISBN 978-1-927339-89-3

CAUGHT IN BLACK HEADLIGHTS is Copyright © 2024 by Adam P. Fuchs. All rights reserved, including the right to reproduce in whole or in part in any form or medium.

Published by Coscom Entertainment

Text set in Garamond
Printed and bound in the USA

Cover design and interior photography by A.P. Fuchs

This book was written in memory of Gord Downie.
Poet. Songwriter.
Inspiration.
Canadian.

CONTENTS

Introduction	i
Where Did the Sunshine Go?	1
That Cold Chatter	3
My Secret	5
Vaporizer	7
Deviation	9
Tub Alone	11
What's it Take?	13
Bricks	15
Inked	17
Unknown	19
The Hard Sell	21
Mindful Vindicting	23
Burn this Mother Down	25
Think it Through	27
Four-panel Bewilderment	29
In Dark	31
Aspirations	33
Four-panel Double	35
In Line	37
Finality	39
Doing Time	41
The Bottom	43
Fairytales No More	45
Non-disappearance	47
Life's a Smoky Cigarette	49
Inside	51
Working All the Time	53
What is Death?	55
Stuck	57
Fin	59

Taste	61
R.I.P.	63
Sunk	65
Ignore All You Know(?)	67
Sleep	69
Naked Heart	71
Unmet	73
Can't	75
Dammit	77
Balance	79
Spherical	81
Early	83
Thud Thud Thud (Parody)	85
Piano Man	87
The Shave	89
I am Fade	91
This is it (It's All Going Down)	93
Don't	95
This is the Job	97
Choose	99
Finale	101

CAUGHT IN BLACK HEADLIGHTS

Introduction

This book has been a long time in the making. Years, in fact. In the old days, I'd regularly write poetry alongside my fiction, but then came a time where I didn't really have much to say poetically. I had already exhausted my heart with pouring out laments on love and loss through *The Hand I've Been Dealt* and *Still About a Girl*. I went to the dark side with *Haunted Melodies and Other Dark Poems*. But this . . . this book is different.

This book is about life, its questions, its observations, its moments, and all the muddy gray in between. I didn't want to write about love and how much it can give life as much as it can take it away. I didn't want to write about the monsters under the bed either.

But I had to express. The songs, the rhymes—they all built up and needed an outlet.

What you're about to read are poems meant to be contemplated. Some, perhaps, agreed with. Some, perhaps, not, but either way, they're meant to be thought about and reflected back on the reader for their own musings and thoughts.

For the first time in any of my poetry books, this one has a photograph for each poem. A mood-setter, if you will. At the same time, I also encourage you to block the image and cover the page and simply let the words speak to you however they may.

This is life. We've all got one.

Sometimes, it's very bright.

Sometimes, we're caught in black headlights.

- A.P. Fuchs
The Central, Manitoba

A.P. FUCHS

CAUGHT IN BLACK HEADLIGHTS

Where Did the Sunshine Go?

Where did the sunshine go?
Did it hide behind your wall?
Those rays of timber and lightning,
Once so big, so tall.

Where did the sunshine go?
Did it go infrared and unseen?
Once so bright and so strong,
Did it become calm and serene?

Where did everyone go?
Did they move to yonder and past?
How did I wind up so alone,
Here, with no chance to last?

Where did the sunshine go?
Your blinding star of gold?
Did you sneak it away to your castle of ice,
Only to be blue, and frozen and cold?

Where did the sunshine go?
Where is it?
Where did it go?

A.P. FUCHS

CAUGHT IN BLACK HEADLIGHTS

That Cold Chatter

Tonight it's all icy and cold.
Life locked up,
All in a frozen storm.

Wind howling
And blowing through you,
The kind that permeates the bones.

Ice cubes and winter trails;
Snow-covered nitroglycerin in tanks
Makes for a heart of sleet.

"Put me out in the thaw," he says.
"There's a sun coming up over the horizon."
Except the pain is a million miles away.

Trembling hands and stiff arm movements
Are the trademark of the day.
You know the one: That cold chatter.

Body chatter.
Cold knees
And frozen toes.

He's not going anywhere tonight.

A.P. FUCHS

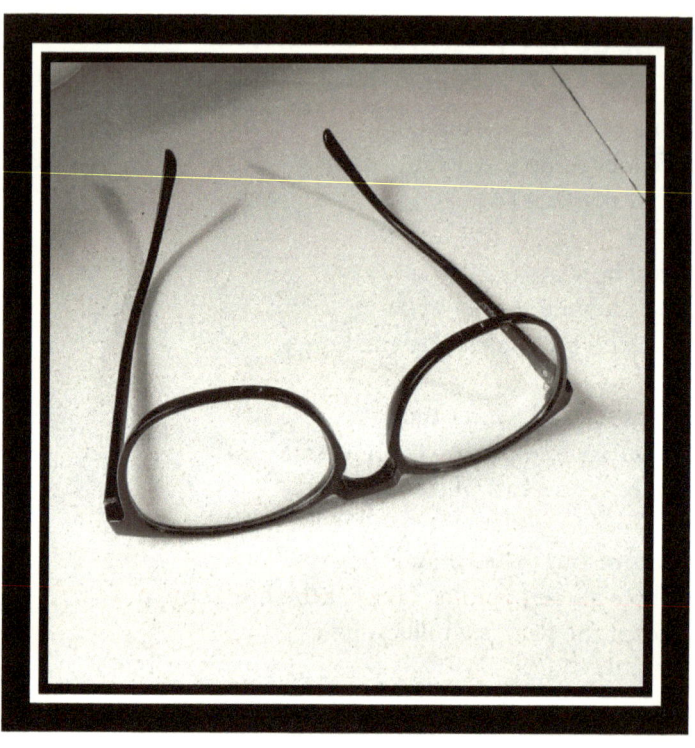

My Secret

No one knows what I've gone through
And neither will you.
Quite frankly,
You'd never believe me.

A.P. FUCHS

Vaporizer

Don't stand over there,
Alone.
Come vape with me,
'Cause maybe then we'll see,
We'll both enjoy rich vanilla together.

Don't look over there
To home.
Come stand with me,
'Cause maybe then I'll see
We're not enjoying rich vanilla at all.

Perhaps you breathe deep strawberries.
Perhaps my vanilla's gone dry.
Perhaps it turns out I'm very
Your very sort of guy.

Just don't stand over there,
Alone.
Come vape with me,
'Cause maybe then we'll see
We'll revel in these steam clouds together.

Vaporizers
Vaping,
Vaporizers
Escaping,
Escaping,
Escaping.

A.P. FUCHS

Deviation

I hate to say it,
But the Christians
Got it wrong.
They put the law
Above the person.
That's not
What Jesus did.

A.P. FUCHS

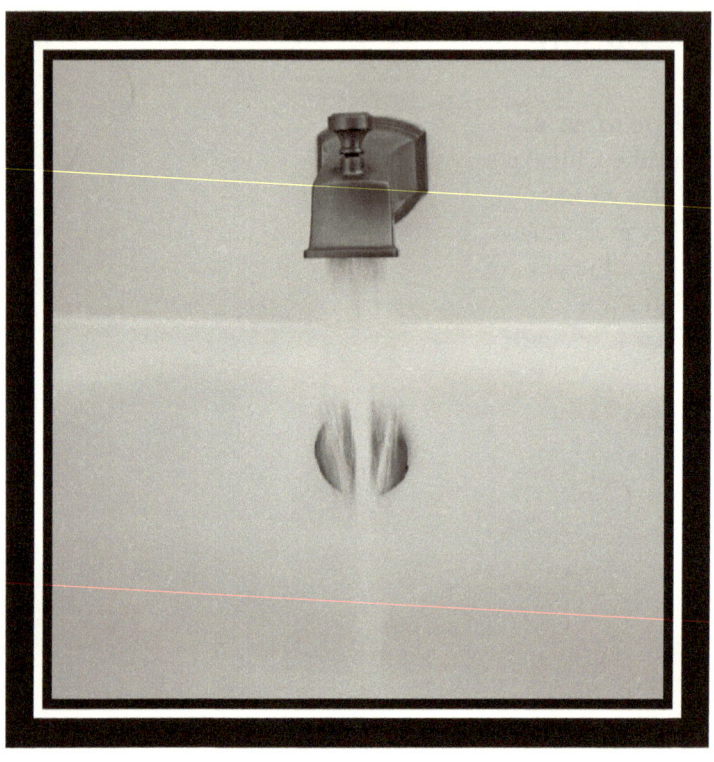

CAUGHT IN BLACK HEADLIGHTS

Tub Alone

There was that time
I was in the tub,
Water to my knees,
A cigarette
Making ashes,
Dangling from my mouth.

The music went loud
From the stereo on the floor
And I could still hear it
With water around my ears,
Cigarette above the water line,
Dangling from my fingers.

That was that time
When I was truly alone.
How did I get here?
Where are you?
Where am I?
But here,
Dangling,
Barely hanging on.

What's it Take?

What's it take to be a writer,
To be on the map?
What's it take to be a writer,
The kind on your jacket flap?

Pen and ink dribbles,
Pouring from the mind.
Black formations and ripples,
The heartfelt transparent kind.

What's it take to be a writer,
The one you know on sight?
What's it take to be a writer,
The one with notepad manner at night?

Imaginations and word play,
Daring to be true.
Definitions and text days,
Going from me to you.

What's it take to be a writer?
What's it take?
No, really,
What's it take?

A.P. FUCHS

Bricks

People
Build
Resistance
When they know
Something's wrong.

They won't get along.

The
Walls
Grow
Even when they don't know
Something's wrong.

Not getting along.

Until
They
Can
See they never knew
Something's wrong.

And still don't get along.

A.P. FUCHS

Inked

I am a thick, dark line
On life's paper.
India ink
Though Canadian
Jotted
A black scar.

Black sheep,
They say.
Black wool,
No,
Black ink
On your white world.

I'm an em-dash,
The pause.
You hold your breath,
I hold mine
And we see where this black ink takes us.

Away
To a land of ellipses
Because ellipses are safer.
They trail,
They pause,
Not always a grand reveal.

But I haul you back
To my black line.
I am a black line
Drawn in the sand,
Drawn on white parchment
I
Am
Em—

Dashing through,
Dashing you.
Black ink
On your white world.

CAUGHT IN BLACK HEADLIGHTS

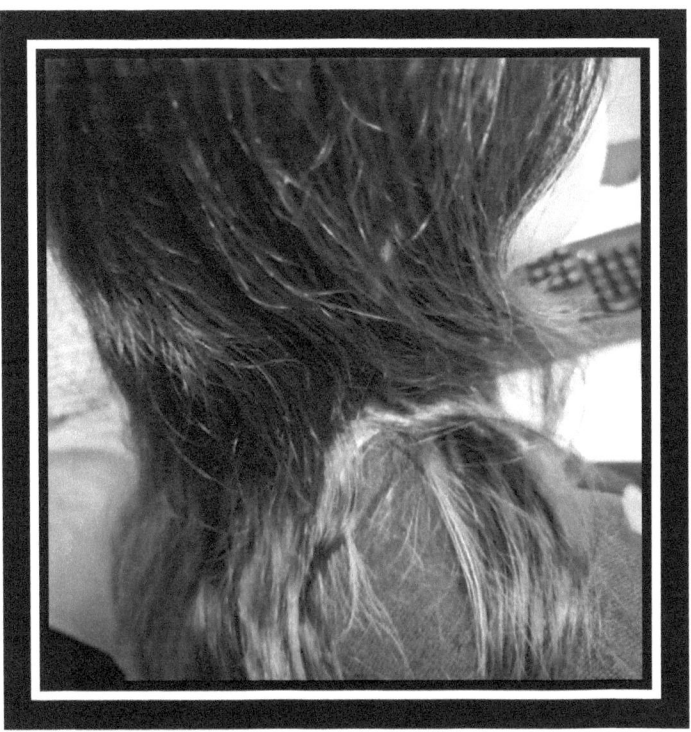

Unknown

Never knew a black girl with ruby-red hair before.

A.P. FUCHS

The Hard Sell

Lonely man at the table,
Hawking wares.
The whole world
Is a flea market
When you think about it.

Sell your smile, sell your face,
Sell your beauty and body language
In peppermint shakes.

Lonely girl in the stable,
Shoveling shit.
The whole world
Is meant for fertilizer
When you think about it.

Sell your words, sell those lips,
Sell your heart and thought patterns
With vanilla fingertips.

A.P. FUCHS

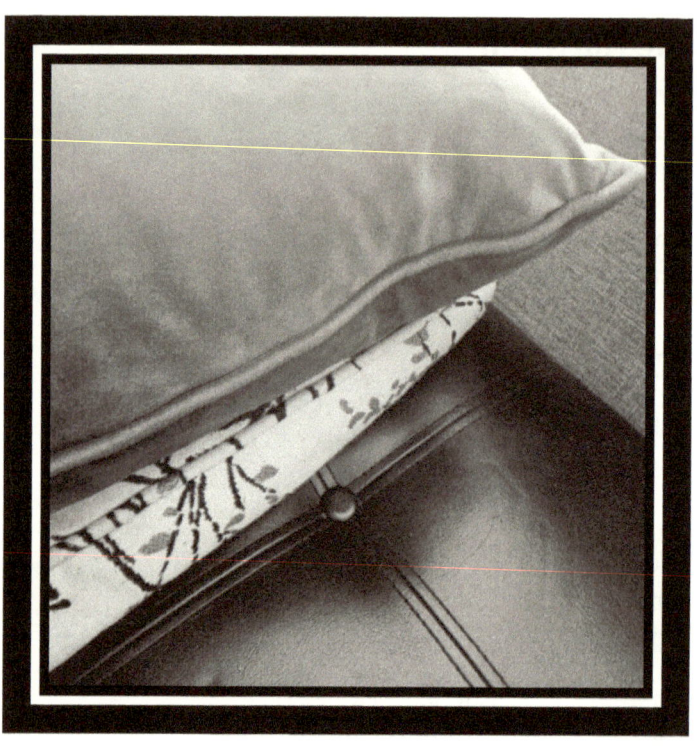

Mindful Vindicting

Pressed for sleep,
Heart awakes,
Brain gone,
Internal Doomsday Clock ticking.

Distance obtained
From life
From dreams.
Spirited disconnection sickening.

Doom and
Gloom
Hollow fortitude
Mire of descent thickening.

Aching eyes,
Exhausted beats
Disappear into the dark,
Emerge in a kind of quickening.

Amidst the smoke,
Amidst the ethereal glow
Of those black headlights
Of mindful vindicting.

A.P. FUCHS

CAUGHT IN BLACK HEADLIGHTS

Burn this Mother Down

"Put the kettle on,"
She says
While I stand in the kitchen.

"Get the oven on,"
She says,
And there I am, just itchin'

To tell her to do it herself.

"We need to drink up this place,"
She says
As I get the water going.

"We need to heat up this place,"
She says
As I get the fire roarin'.

Come here and light 'er up yourself.

But she wants me,
She says,
To burn this mother down.

A.P. FUCHS

Think it Through

A lot of people think it's funny
Chasing after the devil,
Mixing with the occult.
The only problem is,
What do they do
After they've found him?

A.P. FUCHS

CAUGHT IN BLACK HEADLIGHTS

Four-panel Bewilderment

I wonder what people envision
When I tell them
I make comic books?

A.P. FUCHS

In Dark

When all the world is quiet
In the middle of the night,
It is then,
And only then,
That I'm doing all right.

A.P. FUCHS

Aspirations

Everyone wants to be innocent.
Wasn't me.
Wasn't you.
Wasn't us.
Wasn't even them.

Everyone wants to be perfect.
In word,
In deed,
In thought,
In soul.

Everyone wants to be iridescent.
Always me,
Always you,
Always us,
Even always them.

Everyone knows they can't
Always be good,
Always hit the mark.
Effortless effort?
Always a mad dash to maintain.

No one's innocent.
Not me.
Not you.
Not us.
Not them.

No one.

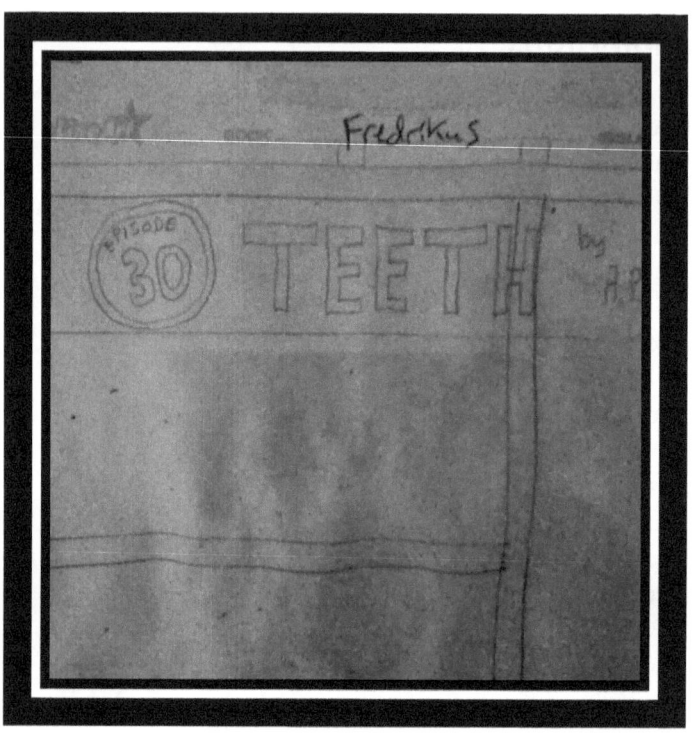

CAUGHT IN BLACK HEADLIGHTS

Four-panel Double

Making comics
At my own book signing,
Working while working.

A.P. FUCHS

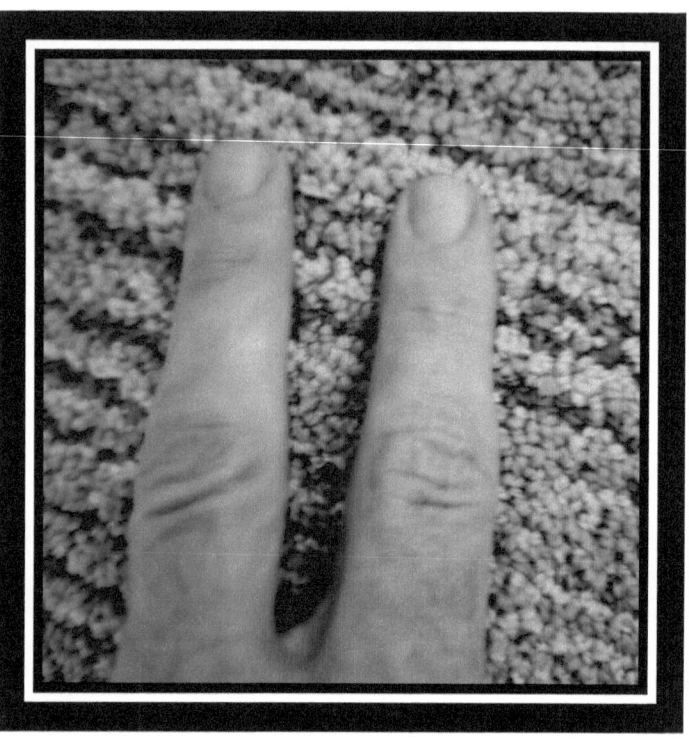

In Line

The thing that got to me
The most
Was our parallels.

A.P. FUCHS

Finality

The world's ending
And no one sees,
No one believes
That we're all done for.

We've gone too far
But won't admit
Nor submit
To our careful wrongs.

Destination inevitable,
Obliteration certain
There, behind the curtain.
Planet Earth complete.

A.P. FUCHS

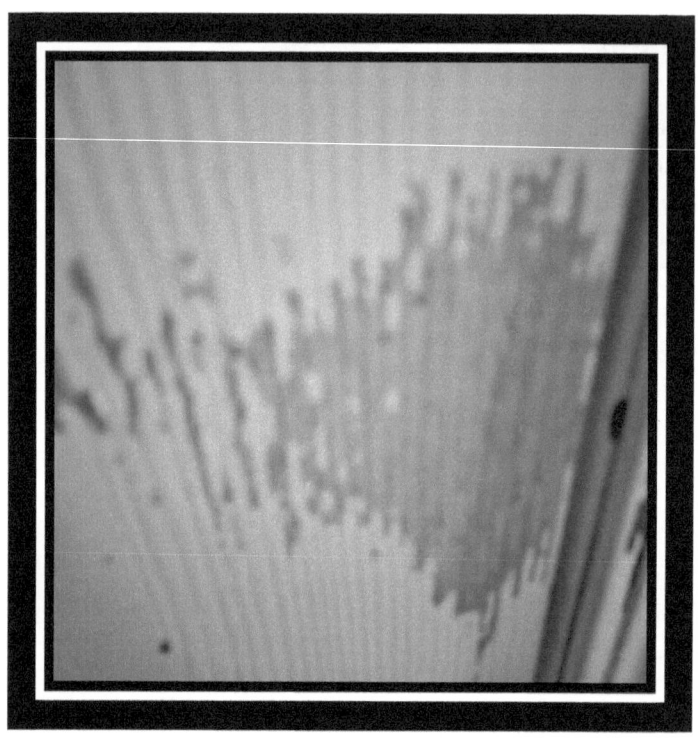

Doing Time

Like a prisoner in his cell, I make scratches on the walls.
And I make my marks
Except the walls are my skin,
Each cut per day I'm alive.

I don't remember my crime
That sentences me to life on Earth.
Wish I could.
Maybe I should?

I'm hoping for a pardon soon.

A.P. FUCHS

CAUGHT IN BLACK HEADLIGHTS

The Bottom

My saddest moment
Was when
I realized
All my pain
For my whole life
Stemmed
From love.

A.P. FUCHS

CAUGHT IN BLACK HEADLIGHTS

Fairytales No More

I don't believe in fairytales anymore.
The very concept means you're keeping score.
Are you there
Or do you still have that place of where's?

You can't hope for the day when
Your current now becomes then.
You cannot hope for the hope's not real.
Never was part of life's deal.

Fairytales and hopeful lies
Are all fine and good until a piece of us dies,
Then we see through the veil and know
Happy endings was just a smoke-and-mirrors show.

Feel that heart sink at that moment of truth.
It's all eye for an eye, tooth for a tooth.
I don't believe in fairytales anymore.
I've lost interest in keeping score.

Goodbye dreams.
Hello screams.
Goodbye to me.
Goodbye . . . just . . . goodbye.

A.P. FUCHS

Non-disappearance

The Internet preserves all memory;
But what if I want to be forgotten?

A.P. FUCHS

CAUGHT IN BLACK HEADLIGHTS

Life's a Smoky Cigarette

Life's a smoky cigarette
In between the days
Of my newfound malaise
And the bottles of whiskey cream.

She pulls me one way,
She pulls me another,
Bonded to each other
And the bed of honey cream.

Life's a bottle of pills.
Two, maybe more.
I think my stomach is sore
During this surreal and unofficial dream.

She said come home.
She said I am your safe place
Away from the race
Of chasing after steam.

Life's a container of pain.
It's all I know.
Torture is slow
With the hope of a happy dream.

End it, I want.
Finally stop the madness.
Finally stop the badness,
That unstoppable evil team.

A.P. FUCHS

Life's a smoky dream.
Life's a thing of do or dies.
Life's a thing of truth or lies
All wrapped in a smoky cigarette.

End it, I said.
Just finish the job.
Finish what's been robbed.
Just . . . no more screams.

No more screams.
No more, please.
No more.

CAUGHT IN BLACK HEADLIGHTS

Inside

I can hear the wind.
Snow on the ground.
Cozy inside.
I am home.

A.P. FUCHS

Working All the Time

Exhausted.
Tired.
Barely holding on,
Working all the time.

Downright fried,
Wrung out and dried,
Not much left anymore
After working all the time.

Life's a haze.
Body broken,
Spirit crushed
From stress and working all the time.

But, you see, it is my doom,
My sadness and gloom
To spend it all
Working all the time.

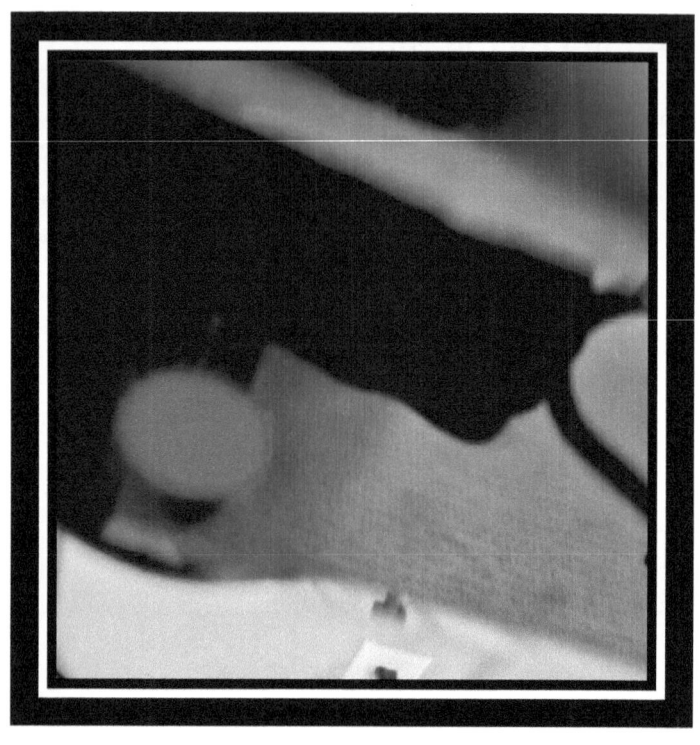

What is Death?

What is death?
A door?
A portal?
An end of one thing
And the birth of another?

What is death?
The dark?
The light?
A changeover of flesh
To spirit and grace?

What is death?
A casket?
An urn?
A time to celebrate
And a time to mourn?

What is death?
All of the above?
None of the above?
Or something new,
Unobserved and untamed?

What is death?

A.P. FUCHS

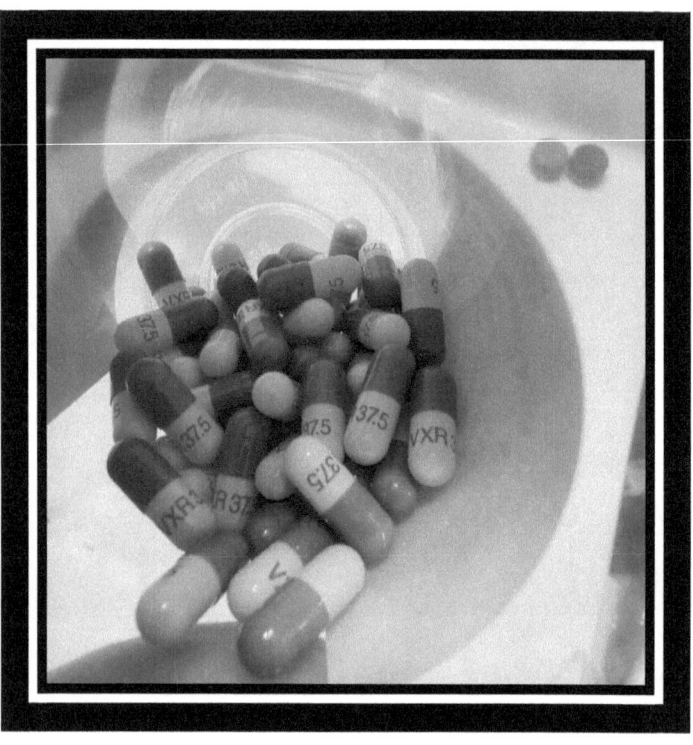

Stuck

Stuck.
Brick in my head,
The inky tendrils of meds.

Can hardly think.
Can hardly cry.
Sleep is what I need,
Goodness knows why.

Stuck.
Sandbag for a mind.
Seems all motivation is left behind.

Need to rest.
Need to crash.
Need to fall apart
In embers and ash.

Frustration sets in.
This is not me.
All I want is to be free.

Stuck.
Boredom.
Dread.
Stuck.

A.P. FUCHS

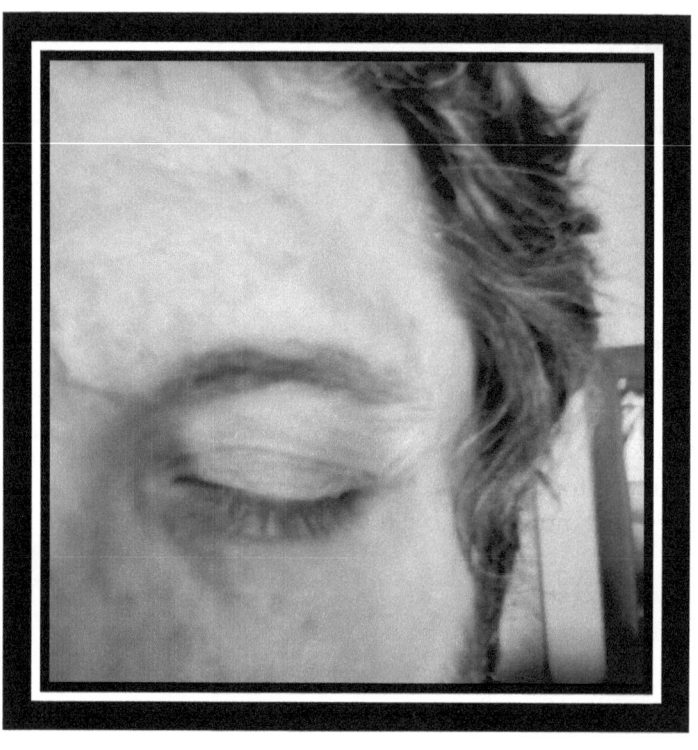

Fin

So tired.

A.P. FUCHS

Taste

Licking the salt
From my wounds
Is like
Licking the acid
From a battery.

CAUGHT IN BLACK HEADLIGHTS

R.I.P.

Were you aware
Of that dare,
You know the one
That cost David everything?

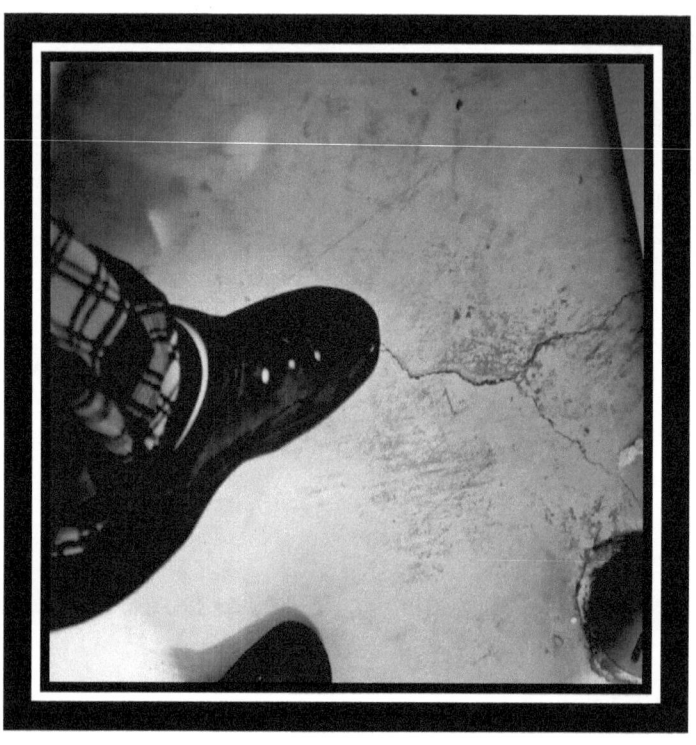

CAUGHT IN BLACK HEADLIGHTS

Sunk

Remember when you could fly
That time,
Doing it all,
Driven,
Pulled through?

Remember when you could swim
That time,
Not drowning after all?
Movement,
Water—pulled through?

Remember when you died
That time
When your world ended, all?
Frozen.
Deceased . . . pulled under?

A.P. FUCHS

CAUGHT IN BLACK HEADLIGHTS

Ignore All You Know(?)

What do you do when you're dealing with poison?
Do you embrace it and let yourself fly
Or do you fall, fall on your back?

What do you do when you're addicted to toxicity?
Do you fall in and live it out without goodbye
Or do you call, call from lying on your back?

How to equate death with life?
How to calculate days left to go?
How to fabricate reasons of strife?
How to ignore all you know?

I do remember disappearing.
I do remember do or die.
I do remember stalling, stalling to say goodbye.

Back under water.
Back to being behind.
Back to the poison,
The poisoning of my mind.

I don't remember knowing all I know.

A.P. FUCHS

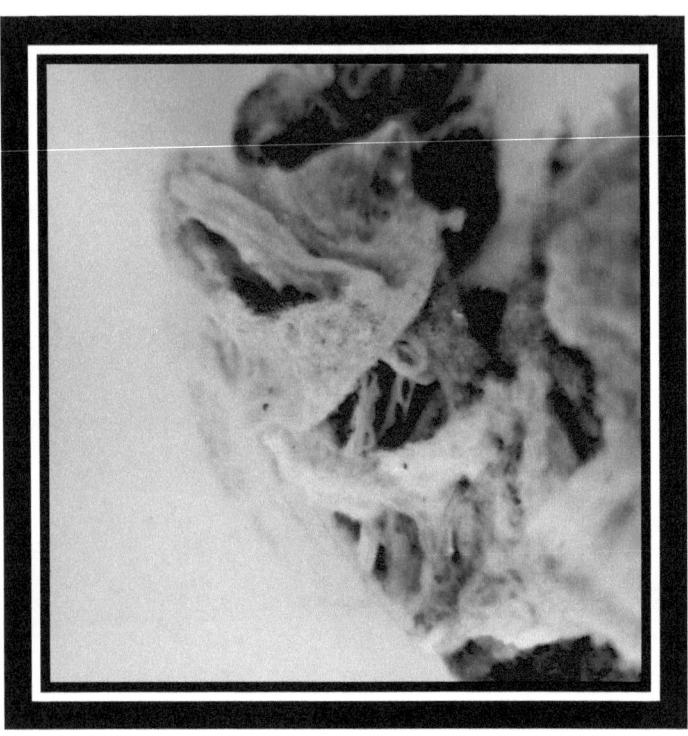

Sleep

It's getting late tonight,
Sleep in the back of my mind.
Back of the head,
Back behind the eyes.

Arms are getting weak with fright.
Fear, there, in the swell of my heart,
The swell of my art,
The swell off the charts.

Want to dose where all is light,
To the right, there, on my side.
There, arms enclosed inside,
Waiting for the enclosure of Sandman's ride.

Want to sleep, just lay tight.
Left to dream.
Left to scream.
Left to a desert's cream.

Sand.
Sandman,
There, in the back of my mind.

A.P. FUCHS

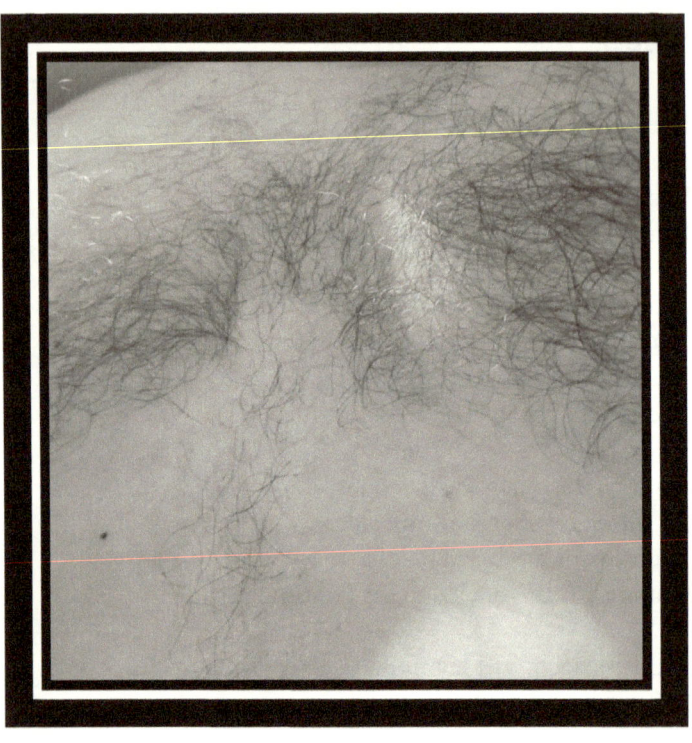

Naked Heart

When you are depressed
You feel undressed,
A naked heart
Taking the spear.

When you're past hurt
And buried in dirt,
A naked heart
Full of fear.

When sadness grips you
And despair seizes you,
A naked heart
All ready to fear.

When death says hello,
You just simply go,
A naked heart
No longer near.

Unmet

For some people
It's impossible
To meet their standards
Even after
You've met them.

A.P. FUCHS

Can't

I remember.

A.P. FUCHS

Dammit

Work,
You stupid computer,
Work!

A.P. FUCHS

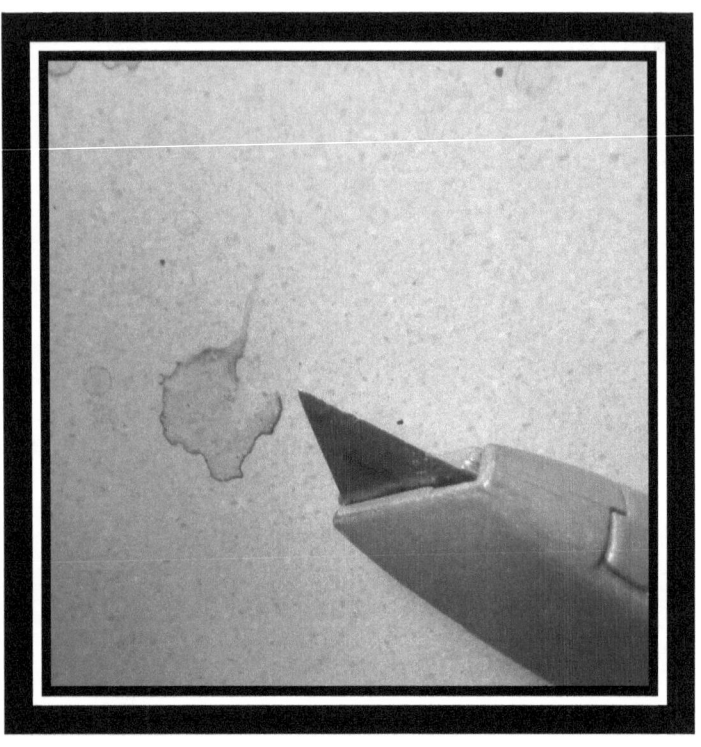

Balance

Walking lines.
Razor's edge.
Teetering
And tired.

Left to the right,
Right to the left,
Balance,
Seesaw.

I see white on my right,
Black to the left,
Darkness behind,
Light in front.

It's a sketchbook
Of lines and point-
Illism.
Yes,
Pointillism was meant to be
Two words.

We are all
Two words.
Right, left.
Black, white.

Pick your opposites,
Pick your side.
Two words.
We are all two words.

A.P. FUCHS

Spherical

Let's go cliché
Of what I'm about to say,
High as a kite,
Feeling all light,
Letting today become yesterday.

Hey, look at that.
I started a rap,
But haven't you noticed
That words get bouticed
So things come out as a snap?

It don't need to make sense.
Rhyming words with itself is nonsense.
But hit those notes
To get those dotes
Straddling there on a fence.

So there it is, my thing to say,
Coming full circle to stay.
Meeting those beats
And climbing those feats
While today becomes yesterday.

A.P. FUCHS

Early

Condensation.
Compression.
8 hours become
5.

Feel fine,
An entire night
In 1 nap.
1.

Doze?
Rest?
30 minutes.
10.

Do what's right:
Heal.
8 hours
But 5.

There's been a change.
Sleep not the same.
7 hours,
4.

Compile and
Squash,
It's all condensation,
Compression.

A.P. FUCHS

CAUGHT IN BLACK HEADLIGHTS

Thud Thud Thud (Parody)

Thud thud thud
Another heart bites the dust.
Thud thud thud.
This anxiety is driving me nuts.

And another thud comes
And another thud comes
Another heart turns to rust.

Thud. Thud. Thud.
Another brain kicks a fuss.
Thud. Thud. Thud.
For a meltdown there is lust.

And another thud comes
And another thud comes
Another heart beats stops its thrust.

Thud. Thud. Thud.

Thud.

A.P. FUCHS

Piano Man

Play me a song, Piano Man.
Play me a song I can dance to.
Play me a song, Piano Man.
You do your part; I'll see what I can do.

Play me those ivories and black keys.
Play me those diaries so I can see.
Play me those jingles and tunes.
Play me a song, away from this maroon.

Play me a song, Piano Man.
Play me a song, I can sleep to.
Play me a song, Piano Man.
You move your fingers; I'll move a few.

Play me those melodies.
Play to me my maladies.
Play to me that ballady
Songs in whole-heart harmony.

Play me a song, Piano Man.
Play me a tune.
Play me a song, Piano Man.
Play me a song for my doom.

A.P. FUCHS

CAUGHT IN BLACK HEADLIGHTS

The Shave

I shave.
I hate it.
Each stroke of the razor
Peeling a little of my life away.

Society's norm,
The men.
We need to be clean-shaven
With bits of ourselves gone away.

The beard is natural.
It's what we produce.
But somehow naturality
Has become taboo.

Sure, some guys pull it off,
The beard.
But they still shave it.
They still shape it.

We all peel our lives away.

Take this metaphor as you will.
Take it with whatever skill,
But know in part
That a beard is art.

Natural depression
Over facial expression
In a clean-shaven world,
Losing ourselves along the way.

A.P. FUCHS

How many blades?
How many times all's abuzz?
How many losses
When we peel our lives away?

No more Mr. Natural.
Only Mr. Supernatural,
Manicured and clean,
Lost to society's norms.

A beard is a good place to hide.

CAUGHT IN BLACK HEADLIGHTS

I Am Fade

A dog, me.
An old dog,
Me.

Middle-aged and nothing
But a cartoon.
A goof.
A screw-up.
You know the word:
Failure.

CAUGHT IN BLACK HEADLIGHTS

This is it (It's All Going Down)

It's all going down,
All ripped and torn.
Life.
It's happening now
And there's nothing you can do about it.

Well, one thing,
When it's all going down.
You could leave, opt out.
The choice is yours.

Could be considered brave,
When it's all going down.
Could also be selfish
When things are spinning around.

But most don't make that choice
And as well they shouldn't.
People need people
When it's all going down.

You are bedrock.
He is sediment.
She is dirt.
I'm the pebbles on top.

That's how it works
When it's all going down.
You have a role.
So do I,
And so does she.

A.P. FUCHS

And he.

So play it up,
Suckers.
Suck it up,
Players.

Step up to the plate,
Watch the pitch.
You need to swing hard
When it's all going down.

CAUGHT IN BLACK HEADLIGHTS

Don't

Never piss into the wind.
Think on it.

This is the Job

Go ahead. Do it.
Do the job.
Be that thing.
Lose yourself.
Work.

Go ahead. Be it.
Do the info.
Be the entertainment.
Unsettle yourself.
Work.

Go ahead. Solve it.
Do the mystery.
Be the resolutor.
Unmask yourself.
Work.

Go ahead. It's not hard
To do the thing
And be that person.
Unravel yourself.
Work.

Get it done.
Go ahead.
Be it.
Do it.

Work.

Choose

Quetiapine
Mirtazapine
Vortioxetine
Take your pick.

Clonazepam
Lorazepam
Diazepam
Make it quick.

Venlafaxine
Desvenlafaxine
Duloxetine
Make it mean.

Be more than
What you seem.
Slowly go
Drift to a dream.

A.P. FUCHS

Finale

And so it ends
Because all things do.
Unravel.
Fall.
All our days marked.

But the end,
The end isn't the end.
Just an unraveling
Of human skin
And thought and words.

Don't be dismayed
When the end comes.
The end is not the end,
Remember?

Think.
Think hard.
You know better
As do I.
Remember.

You need to remember.
The end.
The fall.
The unraveling.

The birth.

About the Author

A.P. Fuchs is the author of over 40 books and the writer-artist of multiple comics. He's been writing and publishing for over 20 years and doesn't plan to stop any time soon. When he's not writing, he indulges in video creation and visiting the toy store for collectibles and superhero memorabilia.

A.P. Fuchs makes his home in Winnipeg, Manitoba, right in the middle of North America (no, really, go look at a map).

His official website is **APFuchs.ca**

His YouTube channel is **YouTube.com/@apfuchs**

ALSO BY A.P. FUCHS

BLOOD OF MY WORLD TRILOGY

DISCOVERY OF DEATH
MEMORIES OF DEATH
LIFE OF DEATH

UNDEAD WORLD TRILOGY

BLOOD OF THE DEAD
POSSESSION OF THE DEAD
REDEMPTION OF THE DEAD

THE AXIOM-MAN™ SAGA
(LISTED IN READING ORDER)

AXIOM-MAN or
AXIOM-MAN: TENTH YEAR ANNIVERSARY
SPECIAL EDITION
EPISODE NO. 0: FIRST NIGHT OUT
DOORWAY OF DARKNESS
EPISODE NO. 1: THE DEAD LAND
CITY OF RUIN
EPISODE NO. 2: UNDERGROUND CRUSADE
OUTLAW
EPISODE NO. 3: RUMBLINGS
FROZEN STORM (SIDE ADVENTURE)
SCARLET SYNERGY (SIDE ADVENTURE)
OF MAGIC AND MEN (COMIC BOOK)

MECH APOCALYPSE

MECH APOCALYPSE

OTHER FICTION

A STRANGER DEAD
A RED DARK NIGHT
APRIL (WRITING AS PETER FOX)
MAGIC MAN (DELUXE CHAPBOOK)
THE WAY OF THE FOG (THE ARK OF LIGHT VOL. 1)
DEVIL'S PLAYGROUND (WITH KEITH GOUVEIA)
ON HELL'S WINGS (WITH KEITH GOUVEIA)
ZOMBIE FIGHT NIGHT: BATTLES OF THE DEAD
MAGIC MAN PLUS 15 TALES OF TERROR
UNDENIABLE
THE DANCE OF MERVO AND FATHER CLOWN
FLASH ATTACK: THRILLING STORIES OF TERROR, ADVENTURE, AND INTRIGUE
GIGANTI-GATOR DEATH MACHINE: TRIPLE FEATURE
ZOMTROPOLIS: A RECORD OF LIFE IN A DEAD CITY

ANTHOLOGIES (AS EDITOR)

DEAD SCIENCE
ELEMENTS OF THE FANTASTIC
VICIOUS VERSES AND REANIMATED RHYMES: ZANY ZOMBIE POETRY FOR THE UNDEAD HEAD
METAHUMANS VS THE UNDEAD
BIGFOOT TERROR TALES VOL. 1 (WITH ERIC S. BROWN)
BIGFOOT TERROR TALES VOL. 2 (WITH ERIC S. BROWN)
METAHUMANS VS WEREWOLVES

Non-fiction

Book Marketing for the Financially-challenged Author
Canadian Scribbler: Collected Letters of an Underground Writer
Look, Up on the Screen! The Big Book of Superhero Movie Reviews
Getting Down and Digital: How to Self-publish Your Book
The Canister X Transmission: Year One
The Canister X Transmission: Year Two
The Canister X Transmission: Year Three
The Canister X Transmission: Year Four
The Canister X Transmission: The Long Year Five

Poetry

The Hand I've Been Dealt
Haunted Melodies and Other Dark Poems
Still About A Girl
Caught in Black Headlights

www.APFuchs.ca

www.ingramcontent.com/pod-product-compliance
Lightning Source LLC
Chambersburg PA
CBHW060532080526
44586CB00012B/714